CW00337105

THE GOLDSMl

The Goldsmith's Apprentice is Keith Chandler's first collection since moving to the West Midlands, an area which, with its industrial and craft heritage, has influenced many of the new poems.

As Will Daunt has written in Envoi: "In his craft, Chandler has been patient rather than prolific and is the better writer for it. He has been uncompromising in the development of a style that is literate as it is accessible. He deserves an ever-expanding readership."

Previous Publications

in *Ten English Poets* (Carcanet 1977)

Kett's Rebellion (Carcanet 1982)

A Passing Trade (O.H.P. 1992)

A Different Kind of Smoke (Redbeck 2000)

The English Civil War Part 2 (Peterloo 2008)

The Grandpa Years (pamphlet, Fair Acre Press 2014)

Some Responses to *The English Civil War Part 2*

And now, with a fanfare, comes the Court Jester, Keith
Chandler, though as good jesters do he speaks
unwelcome truths. Read this hilarious and mordant book.
Peter Scupham, Poetry Review

A spellbinding book – tremendously impressive,
entertaining, moving, funny. And original. These poems
are always 'about' something.
Anthony Thwaite

His angle on the world is often fresh and funny, equipped
with formidable confidence in the face of uncomfortable
truths.
Rennie Parker, Critical Survey

Various poems here pick up quirky habits and actions,
always with a smile towards our weaknesses. A stunning
group of concentration camp poems are as moving as any
I have read on this subject.
Ann Born, Poetry Salzburg Review

It is a humane, funny, sometimes biting, very English
collection, with a strong apocalyptic theme running
through ... A genuine poet, remarkable for his acuteness of
observation and unshowy craftsmanship.
George Szirtes, Poetry Review

Some Responses to *The Grandpa Years*

In these wry reflections on aging and mortality, Keith Chandler confronts us with a vision that is by turns brutally honest, wise and comically anti-heroic. 'Rewind' is a tour de force in which the poet convincingly imagines the experience of regression to the womb.
Jeremy Page, The Frogmore Papers

There are serious questions running through this pleasing pamphlet, such as why it is that we become besotted with toddlers. It is these questions and the recognition of mortality that elevates this sequence from a private tribute to a life event into a lyrical consideration of change and time.
Jan Fortune, Envoi

There are strong poems here on the black comedy of aging and consolations to be found in the company of grandchildren, but Chandler is best when writing about the invisibility of the old. The title poem is a wonderful answer to Larkin's 'Toad's Revisited'.
Andy Croft, The Morning Star

The Goldsmith's Apprentice

Keith Chandler

 Fair Acre Press

First published in Great Britain in 2018
by Fair Acre Press

www.fairacrepress.co.uk

A CIP catalogue record for this book is available from the
British Library

ISBN 978-1-911048-28-2

Printed and bound by Lightning Source

Lightning Source has received Chain of Custody (CoC) certification
from:
The Forest Stewardship Council™ (FSC®)
Programme for the Endorsement of Forest Certification™ (PEFC™)
The Sustainable Forestry Initiative® (SFI®).

Front Cover Image: 17th Century Goldsmith. Anonymous.
Nurnberg.

Typeset and Cover Design by Nadia Kingsley

Acknowledgements

Thanks to the editors of the following magazines and anthologies in which poems have appeared: Envoi, The Frogmore Papers, The Interpreter's House, Much Wenlock Festival Anthology, The North, Poetry Review, Obsessed with Pipework, The Poetry of Staffordshire (Offa's Press), Poems about Birmingham (The Emma Press), Wolf Hoard (The Border Poets)

The following poems have won prizes in competitions: Chemo Nurse (Much Wenlock Festival), Ties (Ledbury), Knitting (Wells), BVM blues (Ver), Travellers (Ware), Old Man at the Gym (Torbay), The Goldsmith's Apprentice (National Poetry Competition 2012), Upper Slaughter (Edward Thomas Society)

Thanks to The Border Poets and Bridgnorth Writers for their encouragement, to Paul Francis and Jeff Phelps for their help with this collection, and especially to Nadia Kingsley for her skill and enthusiasm in "making it happen."

For Vic

with love as ever

Contents

The Goldsmith's Apprentice

You will change into 'trashers', canvas shoes,
when you lock yourself in at eight.
Collecting your strongbox from the safe
it will be weighed. It will be weighed again
when you clock off at six.
You will sit at a vice with apron attached
to funnel the filed off dust.
You will blow your nose into newspaper
and not put grease in your hair.
Similarly, when you swill your hands
(your lunch box having been inspected)
it will be into this tank of sawdust
into which you will also expectorate.
All these - shoes, clothes, snot, sawdust -
will be burnt off at the end of the month
into a rough bar called an 'elmer'
worth more than you earn all year.

In return we will teach you to saw and buff;
to solder, blowpipe dangling from your lip
like a forgotten cheroot;
to cast by 'lost wax method'
rings and brooches, each mould unique
then melted out, weeping fat tears;
to hammer flake so fine
it will float like a feather above your face;
to draw out wire for filigree work
shinier than a girl's hair, stronger than her love;
to forge, clinging like slinky fingers
to Beauty's neck, chains so slim
no one but yourself may see the links.
You will breathe this atmosphere of dust
and soft percussion, dying at last
stoop backed, purblind,
your lungs lit up like a golden branch.

Coalport Girls

Who like you
could magic up, plate after plate,
the fuzz of peach, the frosty glow of grapes?
Or put a tear drop on the peony's cheek
fresh as your own
wet from the fields of Shropshire or East Wales?
Or paint to order a bouquet of birds,
the colour not yet faded from their necks?
Lips blue with cobalt and with cold,
brush hairs spit-licked to a point,
could gild a rim, so trimly roundelled
no Lady might detect its true beginnings,
then replicate her new escutcheon
on cup and saucer, creamer, bonbon dish...
I have seen photographs in faded sepia –
your beauty bundled up in man-sized aprons,
seated at trestles, piecework piled high
behind, in front, like tower blocks;
or on a charabanc outing to Llangollen,
bolt upright in your Sunday collars,
hands tight-gripped against unbusyness,
and wondered at the tiredness of your smiles.
But not as pale as on that black-edged day
a row of lodgings, undermined,
spilled casually downhill toward the Severn.
When they dug you out, your upturned faces
and clay filled mouths, wide open gazes
once glazed the colours of a summer morning,
now whitish grey –
dull as the slipware before it is ghost fired.

Glassworkers, Amblecote

See them - old men in braces, a team of four
in darkness shaped like a bottle oven
lit by flares from the gloryhole - a roar
when it opens, otherwise a throttled purr

like snoring. Each knows his place.
The Footmaker's job's to gather glob,
not white- nor red- but toffee-orange hot,
on the blowpipe, fluid but not too wet

for the Servitor who starts the endless turning
on the marver, back and forth, begins to blow
breath-bubble, cupping it into shape
like a woman's breast, before handing it on

to the Gaffer, the only one allowed to sit.
Turning it round, he widens out a lip
with tweezers. Dipped, redipped in heat,
measured, refined... finally he nods, snips it off

for the Taker-in, who tongs it to the lehr,
the cooling shelf, to skin over, anneal.
What happens thereafter, whether cut or graved,
is not their business. Each seems content

to be part of the chain, to pour with amber sweat,
to shout gently, fag up over tea,
to keep the punty rolling, centred, never to break
or drop glass tears. Never to grow rich.

Clarice

Where did they come from,
those hot hot colours -
tangerine, cadmium, jade, cobalt...?
Those tom-tom patterns, stripes and triangles
jiving together, melt-down shapes?
Not from the monochromes of Tunstall,
its pot banks, back to backs,
factories like prison hulks.
Not from the family chain-linked
to poverty, childbearing, hard work.
Not from the fashionable post-war demand
for 'best' china, rose sprigged trellises,
all that was 'posh', little finger dainty...
Where did it come from, your fierce originality
(and you so shy, unlike your signature
with its cursive *Look at me* loop the loops)?
Where, given half a chance by A J Wilkinson
to decorate his rejects, his spoilt seconds,
did you find, home girl, such bizarre landscapes?
Clarice, I see you as a child sent out with a pram,
little brother at either hand,
to scavenge for coal among the cinders
and muck of some nearby shord ruck,
flask shaped chimney and oven mouth
flaring behind, finding instead
shards of beauty, sharp edged colour -
copper, emerald, coral, azure -
piecing together the jazz-age modern
out of the smashed up past.

Elkington, the gold-plating man

At first a fairground huckster:
Bring me your pins, your toys, your trinkets
See them transmuted before your eyes
you soon had the sass, the nous,
to limit your invention to *'articles of taste'*.
Salvers. Vases. Presentation cups.
Electroplating – the artistic rage!

On a tour of New Hall's bubbling tanks
you presented Prince Albert
with a gilded rose –
so 'real' its dewdrop, spider web,
he wanted to hold his breath.
Centrepiece of the Great Exhibition
your version of the Cellini salt.

Later, keen to extend your profit,
factories began to churn out
cases of fish knives, doorknobs, taps.
But unlike real gold which ever after comes
fresh as a daisy out of the ground
in time your applied molecules
of magic began to wear thin

leaving millions of customers
with tarnished goods in their hands
and the unemployed,
your ten warehouses closed down,
hunched on sunset benches,
the gold leaf of nicotine
pinched between finger and thumb.

The Glass Eye Fitter

has stacks of them, pulls them out
tray after tray, like an obsessive collector
of shells. Plastic, not glass, in fact.

Blues, greens and browns. Racked by sizes.
One cabinet is 'Hazel'. Another 'Ethnic'.
Pupils range from pinpoint to belladonna.

He holds them up, propped between thumb
and forefinger, as if plumped between eyelids,
to your cheek, to find the best match.

Shell chosen, he grinds and grinds it
to the contours of a particular socket
like a key cutter. Taking trouble to buff

the edges smooth as an oyster's lip
he makes the best of a terrible job.
As to the wound of "what really happened",

tumour or car smash, he never probes,
but brings the thing up to his own level
again and again, squinting like an artist

to make it better. If it strikes him as odd
to be faced all day by half comic masks
like a Bafta award, he never says.

Nor does he, as strangers often will,
doubletake, patching it over with a laugh.
The old are easiest. They have given up

hoping for much, can turn a blind eye
to their glaring manhole. But the young
are a challenge. Getting them to sit still

for a start. Knowing he can never re-make
that merry glint, bright depths of colour.
Some things – most things? – he can't put right.

Chemo Nurse

How wonderful you are, bursting late
into this waiting room of politeness and fear
with its Hello/Country Life fantazines,
discreet fliers *('How to Stay Positive')*,
help groups, homeopathic diets
and Chapel "just along the corridor"

without apology showing everyone
with a *'TA-DA!'* whisk of your ocelot
the ladder running up your inside thigh
announcing without tact or holdback
in a half Brummie half Jamaican accent
how lucky it was you wore knickers today,

taking by the hand one by one
the women in not quite convincing wigs
or bald as an egg or surreal woollen hats
towards what you call your *'milking parlour'*,
talking nineteen to the dozen so they hardly notice
being rigged up to the poison drips,

talking nineteen to the dozen about the daughter
you left (late again) at her first school,
managing even among the moon-faced
and eyebrowless to raise a smile,
fitting the needle so they hardly notice
how difficult it is now to find a vein.

In this palace of fake cheerfulness
with its wipe clean smiles and flower prints
and a chaplain who asks if there is anything
all morning I hear naughty laughter
billowing out from behind the screens
and think: yes, you are The Real Thing.

Old Man at the Gym

Look at you - puffed out, man boobs juggling
without the benefit of a sports bra,
trying to keep up with that bronze god
gliding beside you, marking time
as on the eternal round of some Etruscan jar -
where do you think you're going?
Careful you don't give yourself a heart attack
as behind you in the wall sized mirror
some ponytailed leotard
climbing onto the weights bench
with thighs astraddle leans back...
Idiot! Do you think she notices you -
dribbler creeping in and out of the Gents?
If she does it is inwardly to smile
at the paunched posture, tonsure patch
which with a Number 2 crop you hope to disguise.
With your iPod, your Nikes, your Go Faster stripes
who do you think you're kidding?
Row hard as you can, shrunk shanks trembling,
you will never turn the river back uphill.
Ride those pedals; rising out of the saddle
and peleton, surmount the Col du Ventoux
in some fantastic Tour de France -
old man, you are going nowhere fast.
Pound the rolling runway, you will never outrace
one who (like the skeleton
inside you, fit as death)
will be waiting with something like a grin
and thermal blanket when, far from plaudits
or medals, finally you run out of breath.

The Skylight

I wish I'd woken you last night
to show how, out of a cloudless sky
of clearest blue, a huge white moon looked down
through our skylight. Not only that
but as the frost got to work
I watched it begin to creep across
like bacilli on a petrie dish
then a blanched fringe of William Morris fronds
until, what with that moon behind like a searchlight
refracted off a billion prisms,
I could imagine anything -
ice caves, escaliers, seraphim
of the four-, even six-winged, kind
covering their faces before a crystal throne
singing *Hallelujah! Hallelujah!* Silently, of course.

But this morning it has all gone -
just the usual fuzz of condensation,
a few dark snail tracks skittering down.

For a day or two

I'd like to have a go at being a woman.
Don't get me wrong. Nothing kinky.
No dressing up – frills furbelow froufrou
drag queen stuff. No nothing like that.
But soft, warm, pleasing. For a day or two.

I'd like to feel how it feels - physically I mean -
to have those bits that bump up and down
when you run. Skirts that go *phew phew*
at the knees. To act flop-eared from the wrist.
Even to have periods. For a day or two.

I'd like to be charming and beautiful
for a change. To sense when I enter a room
those LOOKs. Like that actress I once knew
I'd hide my scorn beneath lowered lashes
and pretend laughter. For a day or two

what a relief not to be led by my cock,
testosterone clock. Not have to be Boss;
Mr Big; one who knows what to do:
make money; take control; lay down the law;
be strong; be a Man. For a day or two

I'd simply waft around the kitchen
in a sarong listening to Woman's Hour
feeding herbs into a gently throbbing stew...
What else? Spot of ironing. Pushing a broom.
Yes that would be nice. For a day or two.

·

Chance

What on earth? Across the Severn
high against the gathering night
a flotilla of lights flashing in time
like a Christmas decoration but flying fast.
Then we saw: a distant skein of swans.
Must be. Not the garrulous honking of geese
but silent, a UFO. Not landing lights
but the repeated upbeat of wings
catching the last of a dying sun.
On off...off on...
Beauty pulsing into the dark.
What kind of luck
could bring such phenomena together:
sunset; distances from and between;
synchronised strobing of wings?
What kind of luck could bring home to me -
obtuse, short sighted as I am -
you who notice such things?

My Other Wife

Have you met her? Look, I click my fingers
and here she comes, gliding as if on castors.
Yes, a stunner. Great cleaner. Superb cook.
Serves up exactly what (and when) I want.
Sausages, chips - she cuts them to fit
bite-sized into my particular mouth.
Do you like? Yes, circa 'Top of the Pops'.
Velveteen shorts and thigh high boots.
Chose it myself. Blonde hair. Orange eyes.
No, not a combo you come across much
but the thing is she will keep those looks.
Feel that. No flab or sag. Pure rubberite.
She can mix then serve ten different drinks.
A variety of sex acts available à la carte
and on the spot. Perfection, is she not?
A doddle to get on with. Likes what I like.
No fighting for the remote in our house.
Never sulks. Or nags. None of those jobs -
Fix this or *Why didn't you?* None of that.
No opinions. No pretence at knowledge.
Is programmed always to back me up.
Does it get boring? Sometime I confess
I pick an argument for the fun of it -
to see her confused, circuits flummoxed.
But Master, Master she pleads backing off
with that cutesy fake American accent.
Sometimes I wish those eyes would fill up
with something like tears. Or just reproach.
Then I go looking for my other Other Wife...

Emmanuelle 2

Wasn't supposed to be like this.
Once upon a time I was the one
chosen to be Mary holding the lamb,
the one with looks filmstar enough
to make the front row mums go *aaah!*
rolling their eyes like a fake orgasm.
The cutest angel with tinselled noose
nodding ahead. The best behaved one.

Shoe-horned into jeans I was the one
the boys wanted. Not really to help
with my homework. Not really to kiss
in a 'nice way'. Not really as 'friend'.
The one with The Body. Great Tits.
The one to tick off their sticky lists.
Succubus of the semi-dark. One hand
in the popcorn, the other up my blouse.

Where did my story board go wrong?
The Missing Father? The Older Man?
The Failed Marriage? At eighteen
nothing to sell but a bored Come-on
when Man-from-the-movies gave me his card
it was (of course) for non-speaking parts -
Sexy Nurse, Woman Pushing Pram,
Passerby acting her pants off.

Now this. Red light. Take 2. Again.
Gauze drapes. A raunchy saxophone.
The hackneyed lines. The lack of plot.
With men. Or women. On all fours like a dog.
In 'fun-filled' scripts directed by men
I close my eyes, think back to when
best blue tablecloth on my head
I rocked a plastic Saviour in my arms.

BVM blues

It was nothing like that. If there were choirs
of angels it was more like singing in the ears
of extreme fatigue. If visitors came
bearing expensive gifts, they mostly
got in the way. The birth itself
was hardly immaculate. He emerged -
but where was the midwife? - more like
a mole-rat, or a prize fighter, not a hint
of the divine. About the crib
clung the beatific incense of dung.

So the nights warped into blur -
suck burp wipe suck burp wipe...
The Father conspicuous by his absence,
old Joseph fussing round worse than useless.
And the worrying, knowing
how boys grow up, get into trouble.
The loneliness. If there was a star
it was the ass, his hairy sympathetic face.
If there was a miracle
it was that milk came rushing to my breast.

Knitting

Seeing you trying to hold it together,
fingers fumbling the points like fish knives
to find a way through, to push loose ends
into place; hair atremble
as if wind blown, wet on cheek,
dropped skein
bobbling as if a cat had it

reminds me what I have heard
of the Faeroes. How out on that rock
rain lashed or sitting outside a cottage
in rare sunshine, the fishwives
gathered into what they call a *'Bindaklubb'*
for the endless waiting, knit for their living.
They make, not some generic blue jersey,
but patterns repeating their own story –
that pink cross might be a remembered name
pulled by hawser under his boat,
that purple band a storm
that took the roof of the island off.
They knit on against the dark
needles flashing like gannets diving
into the pursed seines of herring.
So the neat rows with storied colours
like mended nets at their feet pile up.

Dear friend, don't give up.
Keep plying those oar-like needles
into the surf, twining the wool
over and round, guiding it
tight, however rough,
against the maelstrom, the unravelling.

Skipping

Do you remember how you used to skip? she asked
You know the kind I mean where nodding like a horse

*you do a sort of sideways rising gallop, one foot
nudging the other. On and on. Just for the fun of it.*

*It doesn't matter where you go or what others think
and you don't look back. It's like a trance. Nothing*

*matters but to keep that rhythm, that trochaic dance
along the pavement. I used to love skipping once*

she said, looking beyond me with such wistfulness
that, helplessly, I longed to give her back herself

as I saw her then – black pigtails flying, white socks
flipping round her ankles. I longed to take her back

to when she was little, let the wind bounce our hair
and skipping feel that we could skip for ever and ever

National Trust

Let landscape be hoicked into the flies,
woods, lakes, follies wheeled in from the wings.
Let the estate boundary be nine foot walls -
enough bricks for a shifted village
or to keep poachers and hoi polloi without.
Let there be a three storey high portico with columns
as if to say *Those who lived here were giants.*
May their portraits, elongated as by Gainsborough,
hang sneeringly up the main escalier
while the women, identically satinned,
forearms folded, half turn away
to expose peep shows of snowy bosom.
May there be, among later generations,
a wastrel who runs off with a dancer
or (breathe it softly) has a taste for *'the unconventional'.*
May the rooms be too high, the beds too big,
the furniture too Chippendale to be comfortable -
all tasselled off with a rope, a teasel.
Let there be hosts of ghostly servants
lurking invisibly up the back stairs,
in service tunnels or clammy underground kitchens;
others are weeping in the attic.
May there be cabinets of untouchable blue and white,
potpourri in every WC.
Let there be a plant stall and
always, first port of call, an upmarket Gift Shop.
Always in the Tea Room may there be lemon drizzle cake.

Uncle George

is now almost gone from history.
Old photographs show him in the uniform
of a porter, full length apron, oversized cap

hanging back in the station shadows.
George never made much of himself
is the story. *Soft in the head he was.*

Even from this distance you can see
his deference - to the Minor Royalty whose bag
he once carried, to anyone in a top hat.

There are family hints: despite
repeated stroking across the hand
by strap, being cornered in a dunce's cap

like a penitent at the Inquisition,
George never learned to read or write.
I guess he was what we call 'dyslexic' -

saw letters like signals shifting this way then that
in the heat haze shimmying above tracks.
Numbers were the shriek of the London Express

hooting with laughter through his small station
leaving the nerves jumping and jangling
like wayside wires, grit-smuts pricking the eye.

So George waits there in the shadow
doffing his cap, offering to carry your bag,
too shy to ask for a tip, too brutalised.

Aunty Nell

I can see her now, an old old lady
with bead bright eyes, permanent headscarf,
drip at the end of her sharp red nose,

sitting huddled to a banked up fire
in a tiny terraced house in Birkenhead,
the telly (her beloved Corrie) on full blast.

Yes, that was how Nell ended up -
before that, was some kind of servant
given a basement plus cot-sized box

for baby Joan (no father in sight)
in return for donning apron and cap
to come running - *'Modom, you rong?'* -

when Grandmother wanted to impress:
we had a 'maid', push-button bells.
Our house was 'posh', if semi-detached.

Now, sixty years later, I understand
why, poor relation, she was 'taken on' -
mixture of meanness, contempt and shame.

Anyway, Nell, you had your revenges.
Joan a beauty. And such tales to tell
of family black sheep, like Eric-who-drank

and Albert, Grandmother's first husband,
who, shellshocked stammerer, ended up
(whisper it) a lavatory attendant -

how every day you ran with his 'dinner'
carried stork-like in a steaming towel
to the Gents. *'And God help us if it wasn't hot.'*

Looking after Jim

Like an old dog
on a chain every three minutes
the same questions drag round:
Muriel, where is she? Where's Muriel?
It's alright Jim. Muriel has gone to be with Jesus.
Mother, will she be there when we get home?
No Jim, she's also gone to be with Jesus
under my breath *unless she's 127.*
All this while I wheel Jim round
a neighbourhood he can no longer place
so panicked is he by confusion...
that explosion in the engine room
when stationed off Palestine.
Sometimes the thing that keeps him calm
is to sing a half-remembered hymn:
Eternal Father strong to save...
Passers by look at me
as if I was the all-at-sea one.

Stop Thief!

Here he comes, hurtling towards me –
lady in white from Delicatessen
puffing behind - past Chardonnays, Chilean reds,
swinging a frozen leg of lamb

like a Flintstones club.   Clumsy face-off -
list in hand, basket at elbow – long enough
to take in ripped jeans, red baseball cap,
quick eyes - laughing at me it seems -

and to feel... what?   Shit scared, yes;
disgust - *addict! parasite!* -
plus sympathy - the thrill of it,
the nerve of those who have nothing to lose...

and to kid myself - in my rugby days
I'd have tackled him head on,
even now might trip him as he swerves
instead of, with a foolish smile, stepping aside

to see him dodge into the street beyond.
While my heart slows the Manageress comes up
to ask if *Sir* is alright - *That's the second this week* -
and I carry on ticking off my list.

Travellers

I like to see them each year
parked on that half moon of redundant grass
beside the A11, just out of town,
that scattering of flatbeds, trailers, washing lines,
one or two authentic 'gypsy vans'
hobbled skewbald ponies beside...

I know what locals say.
Should get a job. Should clean up
their scrap, their shit. Should pay their taxes
like the rest of us.
How each year, eve of departure,
shed break-ins just happen to happen.

This year nothing. No tyre marks.
No ditched bin bags. Nothing.
Stopping for once I see how someone
(acting on whose behalf?)
has ploughed deep trenches, red clay
welling up through the grass like welts,

and feel not angry, just sad -
that year our cat glaring out of the window
at swallows rebuilding their mud-lipped nest
spooked them so they never came back.

At the Hand Car Wash

Feeling of entrapment
as out of a derelict garage
over-friendly they swarm.
With quick gestures, excitable language,
they remind me of a drive-thru zoo -
that time those too close cousins
teeth bared yanked a wiper off.
Only the Boss has some English.

One waves bucket and squeegee.
Another works a squirty wand
under the arches.
Two more buffet with high pressure jets.
As the windows drip with muddy deluge
I wonder: who are these men?
How did they get here? How do they live?
Hot-bedding in a squat perhaps?

As the suds boil brown then white
I imagine inflatables, sea crossing.
That shadow two feet from my nose
might be someone mouthing for help
waving, clinging to a raft.
All of us thrown together –
myself pampered in faux leather -
by a maelstrom of circumstance.

A couple of rinses the glass
begins to clear. Still not finished
they chamois out the limescale spots.
Perhaps they see themselves
in the future in such gloss?
Then *Ut! Ut! Ut!* Time to escape.
The coins seem so little
but the Boss gives a grin, thumbs up.

Lullaby

Sleep well little bro
in your rucked up red T-shirt,
blue shorts too big,
head to one side, mouth slightly open,
arms straight down by your sides.

No father's hand ruffles your hair
with periodic affection
but final pushes of water,
waves crying themselves dry
on a dirty Turkish beach.

No use murmuring to you
of a make believe world
where the grownups have learned
not to fight. Dream on.
Dream on of a faraway land

where those who are safe and warm
watching pictures on TV
try to be kind, to share
what they can. Something
appears to make you smile

as, turning you over with his boot,
a tall policeman
carries you ashore draped
over his arms like an offering
or like a child deeply asleep.

Upper Slaughter – a "thankful village"

Googling my phone, I read how, almost unique
in England, all twenty-four men of this parish
came back from the Great War alive, unharmed.
Letters *in the event* unopened, sweethearts remet
and married. Officers as well as 'men' returned
to the Big House. Shed door left cobwebbed open
on a row of rigid boots, rakes and hoes
still sloped at arms, no garden went to ruin.
A mother's boy appeared more confident.
A father kissed his first born. No clothes were piled
for the ragman. No spinsters met to knit.
At the school gate a teacher (over age)
returned to cheers where they had sung him off
with *God be with you,* waving paper flags.
The farmer, perhaps scratching his head
over a charlocked field, heard a cheery shout
as, vaulting a gate, his best team came back.
No, nothing lost. Not a limb. Not even a mind.
In Naunton, the next village, where I supped a pint
at The Lion, fifteen enlisted men were killed.
In Accrington, a thousand Pals wiped out...
But just for an hour while the sun shone
on Slaughter, its honeyed stone, its stream
and postcard green, you could believe in myths
of blessedness. For some. The kind of luck
you wouldn't boast, or even talk, about.

The French Wars of Religion

*Mankind, so clever at inventing gods, cannot
reassemble a cloven worm* - Montaigne

Difficult to imagine
sitting in this sunny bastide
how a priest was first broken on a wheel
then crushed beneath the beam of a winepress
his blood gushing like this beaujolais nouveau
I hold spitting and sparking
in a fine stemmed glass to my nose;

or how the Huguenots of Monpazier
and the Catholics of Villefranche, fortified
by strong wine and much singing,
set out by different sunken roads –
it was a moonless night, perfect
for such a raid - to exact revenge
for some neighbourly insult to their religion.

After a night of satisfaction,
tearing down images, both sides returned
crossing, again by separate lanes,
under a light that was increasingly
more like roofs on fire than dawn,
to find their fathers slaughtered, wives ravished,
babes splashed out on cobblestones.

Euro Frisbee

Who started it? After what felt like aeons
of staring out across that forest site
from behind tent flaps; of close avoidance,
stepping around territories as tight
as guy ropes; of clichés in the toilet block:
Wop...Dago...Frog...obsessive Nordic type...
queue-jumping Kraut; of mutual dislike
of cooking smells; of rows then makings up
of Latin lovers humping through the night;
of cross-fire from a dozen Balkan tongues;
of zones where cones discharged the absolute
silence like grenades, twigs went off like guns...
Was it the children, or was it that bearded man
we couldn't place, first took the thing in hand

and sent it spinning? Like a dance, with a flick
of the wrist, high loop, banked elliptical glide
back to the next, so that more – even the Brit –
and more joined in, until that dappled glade
seemed full of leaping, like a lithograph
by Picasso or a playful Swedish film.
Loud too with meaning before the invention of
language - whoops and shrieks. Yes, just a game
of cooperation. But we kept it up –
a secular paten, landmine parcel-passed,
a plastic salver, flying saucer shape
to take us where no war or lack of trust
once was. Till caught up in pine-needled air
like a high-minded sun, we left it there.

Note: 'paten' = a round tray for communion wafers

Two Countdowns

For four maybe five seconds it sat
like a mitred pope, perspiring ice
on its cushion of smoke. At last
storey after storey groping past
like a tower block, spelling out
its name in giant black on white,
A – P – O – L – L – O, it uprose,
sheer demolition in reverse
(and when the sound came back
it was a growl so low you felt
more than you heard the quake
like an underground test) and as
the bonds of gravity fell off
swam clear of earth then, delicate
as a sunflower, turned its face
toward the moon, the quiet stars.

Some late, hurrying to work;
others gathered on the pavement
gasping up, their faces unmasked,
at a skyscraper, silver sheathed
in sunlight, its hernia of flame.
No No No is their silent shout
as for some fifty minutes it sits
on its own future like a judge
until, unforgettable launch
run backwards (and the sky
turns grainy like a TV set
from the sixties) it rushes down
in smooth slow motion like a film
so that one thinks of Babel, Cheops,
all such high hopers, falls to earth
and dust comes boiling up the street.

The Witness
(for Youk Chhang)

As we walked into the countryside
which would make Comrades of us
I abandoned first my books
then my flat-tyred bike then my hopes.
When they began to shoot
intellectuals (those who wore glasses)
I chose to see blurred.
When they accused a child of stealing rice,
slitting open the belly
which turned out to be empty,
I felt sick but showed nothing on my face.
When a couple in our camp had the luck
to fall in love without permission
I was among those who chanted
kill kill kill and cheered and jeered
as they were bundled bound together
alive into one grave.
At the nightly seminars
I was skilled at finding crimes to confess:
Last night I dreamed of noodles, baguettes...
But the killings. There were so many.
In the end they used pickaxes
to the back of the head
because that was cheaper than bullets.
Bodies piled up. Fields of skulls
lying around like rotten pumpkins.
If I failed to fight back or even protest
forgive me.
I am weak. I am human. I was afraid.

The Executioner's Tale *

Pulling the trigger is the easy part.
The worst part is the human touch -
having to lace the prisoner's limbs
to a cross-shaped pole with ropes,
to clasp from behind
with a lifeguard's or a lover's embrace
the underarm stink of sweat,
to see close up the nakedness of the neck
almost wanting to kiss it
as when I dress my own knee-dandled son
guiding a vest down over his head.
Binding the hands
I try to do it gently.
They rarely struggle.
By now their fate
is written in the crossed over
and backward turned palms.
By now it is too late
if they have wet
or even shat themselves.
I don't make conversation
but sometimes murmur
I am sorry it is my job.
Past the waist the hips the knees
trussed in a double helix –
for their own good
to stop them flinching or kicking out –
down to the heels
finished with a hitch, a tethering knot.
The last touch is the blindfold
bound round and round as if for a game
so we do not have to look into the eyes
but at the circle of death pinned over the heart.
Pulling the trigger is the easy part.

*based on the account of a Filipino policeman

43

Death Watch

Knockknockknockknock. Who's there? *Jen.* Jen who?
Genus Coleoptera. Each May the same:
the first warm night - a touch of moon perhaps -
you hear their raps, ripples of ghostly morse,
from room to room; a doctor's listening taps.
Tried everything. Gas snouts from Pest Control
blitzed them with Rentokil. Useless. No good.
Like knocking your own head against the wood
trying to stop them. Sometimes you spot the frass
of new bored holes where they've blundered out
like gunshot. But the bugs, ventriloquists
of beam and joist, have flown. It drives you mad.

Seven years as larvae! Can you imagine it –
such dark determinism, condemned to eat
hard cheese of honey-fungused oak? At last
transmuted to a pupa, a mouse's shit.
But under God, his magnifying glass,
a jeweller's movement – rufous carapace,
clockworking legs. One night you feel the heat,
the call of light, that need to bang your head –
you know the feeling – such longing for a mate,
your own Miss *Xestobium rufovillosum.*
One night! One night! Imagine that slow lust
burning through heartwood like a fuse.

First sex, then death. All must succumb to that
dumb pattern. The frescoed panel, angel face
bitten as if by smallpox – all becomes dust.
It's in the grain. They were already here
in the green wood when the great oak was axed
ages ago. Wedged, split, sawn, augured, adzed...
You can't get rid of them. They're in the plan,
the timbers of the place. The bier. The cot.
So take your time. You'll never root them out.
The sickbed penitent (is it inside his head?)
hears faery carpenters: *knockknockknockknock*...
And when their tiny ticking stops, you're dead.

Lament for a Lost Campervan

Dear Van, where are you?
Like a mother whose child is missing
we catch glimpses of you everywhere.
How proud we were in our Captain Seats
of your shiny newness, on campsites parked
to show off your awning, your customised paint job.
Since then what wonders we have shared
from the temple at Segesta
to the standing stones of Stenness.
True that like us you were getting older,
rusty round the edges, bit Hippy in fact,
but still you gave us the illusion of freedom -
wild camping up mountainsides,
in piazze del duomo, on sodium-lit forecourts,
and once, frighteningly, on a night time beach -
with first light a view of Mont St Michel
the tide rollicking over your hubcaps.
We fitted together so comfortably
like gypsies, or snails in their 'go-faster' stripes.

Poor old Van
what rough men have their hands on you now?
In what knackers' yard in Bilston
are they breaking you up for eBay spares?
Or, sentimental hope, have they done you up
to give pleasure again in some Campervan Heaven -
everlasting picnics in five star lay-bys?
Most probably you have ended up
a giant metal weetabix magnetically hoisted -
our dreams, our history,
our sense of who we are, might be
dropped and crushed, dropped and crushed.

The Hill Walking Club

Where has Bob gone? I hardly knew him
but he was a regular. Every month turned up
with that mocking smile. I can see him now
looking up red faced from lacing up his boots
with an off hand comment. Hardly a friend
I came to like him for his corny jokes
on our uphill slogs. Knew little of his life
or just such glimpses as we allow ourselves
to share with tea and gossip on our halts.
Sometimes these treks into the Borderland
seem pointless. A miserable trudge in fact.
Sleet in your face or sliding down your neck...
Why ever do we do this? I used to ask.
No answer, except perhaps because we can
still get a kind of oxygenated kick
out of our bodies. Plus the odd reward.
That time we stood like Cortés on a peak
and all was gold, gold, gold. Another time
we counted seven fading rainbows parked
as if by some old artist, hoop after hoop.
And once Bob did surprise me, pondering
the chance of other universes ranged
like parallel ridges in the mist... *Or like,*
he said, *those voices that you cannot see*
climbing beside you up a different path.
I knew about his diabetes. And the hip
he expected eventually to be replaced.
But where is Bob? I miss his teasing voice,
his whooped exuberance on a downhill stretch.
And when we close up into single file
to round some col or semi-dangerous edge
I feel the gap in our chain. Getting back
to the cars, it's almost as if I half expect
to see him, having taken a short cut,
perched on the tailgate wrenching off his boots
and looking up with that defensive smile:
So, will I see you guys again next month?

The Fisherman

Whenever I look up
he's there, on the far bank
under an oversized green umbrella
in camouflage trousers and jacket.
All day, through showers
that tin-tack the surface, sun
that burnishes it to brass,
he watches, motionless.

Sometimes he scatters groundbait
with a catapult, sideways flicks,
but mostly his stillness is absolute.
Face and hands backlit
by ripples as from a laptop
he waits for the float to bob under
itself, an exclamation mark,
the line to pull tight.

It must be like that moment
Shelley describes -
the creative mind as a fading coal...
quick! strike! Then the thrill
of pulling something fresh, live,
out of its element
to hold, if only for a second,
like a cupped flame in your hands.

Late Damsons

Unlooked for this late crop
of drupes, almost lost
among the yellow-green cave
of foliage. Blue? More like the wash
on wash of darkness, crimson-black,
of a late Rothko.
Moth-powdery bloom -
each fingerprint
a crime scene where I've handled it.

Swaying, my swollen plastic bag
like a pollen sac, knees braced
against the rails, I reach
and reach into the endlessness...
October blue, frost
at the edge. But those fumes -
of what exactly? Fruitiness yes,
but also something bitter-sharp,
stone at the heart.

Too much too late. Those
I can't reach, tip top ones,
I'll leave for the birds, many
let drop - a treat
for Stripeface who comes snuffling
at dusk. The rest I'll jam
or set to frothing in dark demijohns.
And some I'll press, to knife,
tart cheese, against the curds of white.

And all was for a cherry (Grey Squirrels)

One day green beads
beneath the leaves began to colour up.
Within minutes arrived
grey hordes, wolf shadows, a flying squad.
Starting at the top where no ladder
or thrown stick could see them off,
they squatted, tail over shoulder
like a college scarf, as if to exercise
some ancient right to scoff the lot.

Winter had found them amusing enough -
swimming from branch to branch
tail following behind, a double bounce.
Or hung claw-footed upside down
to get at the feeders, 'squirrel-proof'.
Or, stage misers,
jinking from hidden cache to cache,
their mind a maze of dot-to-dots.
But this... this was too much.

Tree rats the neighbour called them
arriving with his gun.
Pop pop pop. Business soon done.
But thanking him I felt rotten
seeing close up how russet reds
bordered the grey, the bellies white,
tail fur bristled with coppery light...
Chucked on the shed roof
for buzzards to find.

And that cherry crop we'd 'saved'?
Of the branches
low enough to pick, I had,
mouth bearded with juice, more than enough,
the rest let drop, a festering mush.
Come winter, as if to punish us
with a lack of grace notes, leaps and runs,
all music of the trees rubbed out,
we waited, but they didn't come back.

"Whiskers"

What was it – a child's black mitten dropped
at the side of the road? But your mews,
tiny, implorative; big green eyes; claws
pitoning my sleeve, made us pick you up.

No cats I said. But, banished to the shed
in a shoebox, secretly baptised (named
for the cat food advert) bottled, prammed
like a baby... *OK. Just for a week* I said.

So you entwined yourself, subtle as smoke,
into our lives. It is a companionship
suits us both. We let you warm our lap.
You let us tug your ears, tease, sometimes talk

Great Wisdom to. Your role is to amuse –
those pretzel shapes you make when you lick
your behind. You have the feline knack
of never lying down the same way twice.

Your day is spent sphinx-like or elongate
on the sunnier heights. At 8 p.m., kittenish,
your eyes begin to widen, tail to twitch.
Cat flap bangs open. Whiskers is Out!

Not much to thank us for – flea-powdered, fed
out of tins, mostly ignored. But fresh each Spring
with a side-plate of guts your doorstep offering
of **field mice**, fledglings, is devoutly laid.

Now you are getting old, a bit of a grouch.
There is grey in your fur. You sleep more, hate
what you're not used to. We begin to anticipate
how little we will miss you. And how much.

M6 Toll

Travelling North - one sometimes has to -
these days I take the easy route.
Lava flow of log-jammed brake lights
or private carriageway – which to choose?
Paying lip service to my Visa card
the barrier rises in salute.

Flyovered, screened
by alternate rowans, conifers,
places like Burntwood and Brownhills
where you imagine queues of artics
grinding round the A5 fuming
at hold ups, are simply bypassed.

As well as time, it saves the bother
of looking into other peoples' lives -
backyards buntinged
with washing, pallets piled
behind sheds, warehouses
where flat-pack dreams are stored.

If one allows oneself to be passed
it is by Mercs, their windows dark.
The Services, chaired like a VIP lounge,
purvey a superior Cup-a-Soup.
By night you leave Birmingham
to one side, an orange coloured bruise.

So, for some 30 unspeed-copped miles...
till with a grinding of gears and teeth
(*Why can't they all just move South?*
murmurs my Surrey-born wife)
two blending streams of corpuscles,
traffic and motorways re-merge.

Return of the King

When Roy Rogers rode into the Hippodrome
kids from all over Birmingham
its last back to backs, ginnels, stagnant canals,
with pistols from Woollies or shed-carved by dads
thronged in their thousands to thrice daily shows.

When Roy in his fringed white top,
grin apostrophised by dimples, haloed by a Stetson,
Yeehaa-ed old Trigger onto the stage,
kneed the palomino to rear up and "dance"
or folding back rubbery lips to *blow a kiss
to the mighty fine ladies* or to hoof-beat answers
to our called out sums,
we had no doubts. We did not think
that Bullet, the German Alsatian
skilled at finding the farmer fallen off his rick
on Saturday flicks, was one of several hired in.

For an hour all disbelief suspended
and for weeks after, tossing cap onto pegs
like a lariat, we walked tall, walked stiff
bow-legged as if in chaps
soundtracked by the Sons of the Pioneers
with their close harmony jogalong rhythms
Give me land lots of land under starry skies above
blew smoke off the muzzle of imaginary shooters
made bullet ricocheting noises *p-yang p-yang*
as we belly-crawled from rock to rock

until, called in by our mams
from the high chaparall of the bomb sites,
the Trucolor sunsets began to fade,
the grey scale of post war reconstruction,
raw estates, high rise blocks
like flat top mesas in a desert landscape,
road systems like dried out river beds;
plus the exigencies of having to grow up -
outfacing yobs from the secondary mod,
getting up in the dark for a Saturday job -
began to fence us in.

"The fuck off man"

we called him, that shambling freak
we used to follow, at a safe distance,
on his daily drag to the corner shop;

used to imitate, at a safe distance,
his tics and grimaces, head yanked sideways
as by a rope, his hang-dog smile,

jitterbug efforts to cross the road -
stepping out, turning back, stepping out
again, as if to check, recheck himself...

Fuck off! he used to shout *Tits!* and *Penis!*
flinging his arms out like a Welsh preacher.
Then that sheepish wry-necked looking back

with a grin, as if to apologise
for himself, an undeleted mistake.
Come on. Let's follow the fuck off man.

Fuck and *Wank* and *Cunt* and *Courage* –
unspeakable words we hid in ourselves,
longed uncontrollably to blurt

but hadn't the nerve; nor to step solo out
along that sky-wide public pavement
to cross the road, then fifty yards back.

The Sin Eater

Ordinarily they shunned him like the plague -
a shambling heap of hair, half man, half beast;
if met by chance were quick to cross themselves.

But if, say, a young friend was queerly dead
there yet were some - more Welsh than Saxon -
would anguish, *Send, but look not on his face,*

for The Nameless One. Led where a corpse was laid
on the best tablecloth - the only time
that laneward door was open - all was prepared:

the weepers dressed in Sabbath massed around;
a bowl – it must be maple – brimmed with beer
placed in the hands, a *death cake* on the breast.

All tried not to watch as, fiercely urged,
he sipped the ale, chewed at the disc of bread
with sticky saliva sounds, till every grain

(while someone murmured, *Now to thee, dear man,*
be peace. Come not down the lane nor in our fields.
And for thy sins we pawn this soul. Amen.)

each nightdeed, curse, tort, tease, cheat, peccadillo -
and, after, all he touched was tonged then burnt -
was supped or mumbled, every drop and crumb.

Then *(Quick, here come the English priest!)* a fee
of sixpence in his pocket, was push-punched out
to find his way back to the bricked up cave

by a mossy stream. Far from the ways of men
its glimmering water, glints of fish
in amber fly-danced light, its shamelessness.

Mac, 4F, my teaching career

Sir! Sir! Your playground's open! That was Mac
at our first registration. *Look at his flies!*
My job was, I soon learnt, to keep them quiet,
out of The Bossman's hair. Stacking chairs
after Assembly was our forte. We could stretch
that out forever. Then after break – fags
behind the boiler - footy till dinner time...
Never forget the day I took the lot of them
for a Visit. To the Liverpool Tate no less.
Art. What a mistake. By the time I finished
checking them in at the front they were out
the back, lost in the Pier Head tourist chaos.
That was the day I mislaid an entire class
and never admitted it. And they, to be fair,
never let on. A conspiracy between us
not to dob me in.
                           Of all the idiots in 4F
the idiotest was Mac. I can see him now.
Baby blue eyes. Playing the innocent.
Which perhaps he was. *Where's Mac?* I asked
that Monday registration. Sheepish at first –
I wondered why so quiet - their shock came out
in a rush. It seems they'd met up for a drink
in town. Not one to do anything by halves
and egged on by some fellas, Mac had gone on
to drop first speed then acid. Off his head
with paranoia and post-Dali images
had commandeered a car to make it home.
Except Mac couldn't drive. Soon got on to him,
the fuzz. When this blue freak stepped out
of an alley (What was it? Bravado? Panic?
Or just stupidity?) Mac couldn't, didn't stop.
The rozzer who went down never got up.
I only saw Mac once after that. In Styal Open.
A juvenile, and yet they judged him bad enough

for a ten year sentence. A pleasant place.
Coffee machine. Ping pong table. Bean bags.
Much like the day room of the boarding school
I later taught at. Except for that iron grill
behind each curtain.
                              As for myself
I took a different road. Landed a cushy job
in the posh private sector. There I learnt
to keep my feet wiped and my mouth well shut;
to cover up the murder in my heart
for certain senior colleagues. I learned
which parents to suck up to. (*Our kitchen
used to be a ballroom* one young lady boasted.)
Unfair what life hands out. To some good looks,
nice manners, money, brains, style, confidence,
charisma, cut glass accent – the blessed lot.
To others like 4F...
                              There I built up
my pension and my reputation
for respectability.   And the likes of Mac
(A *'Teenage Hoodlum'* the Echo called him)
have put behind me. Out of mind. Almost.

Ties

Look at them. Hauled by the scruff of the neck
from the back of the wardrobe – this rack
of hangman's specials from before I retired.

All sorts. From bootlace to kipper. This one I bought
for 'Bad Taste Day': Mike Myers as Austin Powers
leers crookedly out of a psychedelic mist.

Some try more subtly to be different. Slim Jims
from the eighties: diagonal pastel stripes
that hint at some more arty chap beneath.

But most are boring, boring workaday jobs
I could drag on without giving them a thought -
dark blue with a hint of Old School/Regiment.

What an absurd fashion, these strips of cloth -
fossils, I suppose, from the flamboyant days
of ruff and cravat. A cover up. As if to hide

some tenderness that might unbutton the heart.
Look. My old Interview Tie. Conformity's ID
that says *Yes Sir I will do exactly as I am told.*

These limp rag halters by which I was led
some forty years. And hated most of it.
Day after day, making the sign of the cross

with one of these, a Windsor-style garrotte.
Even now I fear them, find myself
clutching at a top button for release.

Fit of the Giggles

Being invited, for instance,
to contemplate our sinfulness
she'd start us off – elbows,
shoulders beginning to vibrate
along the Mansion polished wood
of the hymnal shelf. No help for it –

the harder you tried or bit your lip
or stuffed a hanky into your mouth –
but to stumble gasping outside.
She would have understood
how today at Yoga for Beginners
on a cold floor at the local Infants'

after an hour of exercise,
breathing deeply, standing on one leg,
being invited by Yvonne our Guide
to contemplate the Chi its golden light...
to RELAX... feel oneself be LIFTED UP...
be AT PEACE with the Universe...

I find myself alone
on a low bench among the pegs
and lockers of a changing room
having laughed till I cried
having laughed till I farted
then splashed cold water in my face

feeling lost
as at the beginning of term
in a new school, no one to share with,
remembering last time I was in church –
my shoulders shake at the thought of it –
I saw her being taken out.

Rewind

It started as, placing some coffee
into the microwave to warm it up,
I noticed the digits instead of counting down
were winding up. Weirder than that
was how in dark glass I saw myself
reaching to take out a steaming cup
except, stone cold, I was putting it back.
OO-CUCK! OO-CUCK! shouted the kitchen clock.

Like those video tapes
you can whizz backwards for a laugh
bowing out of the room
I sashayed, waddling in reverse, to my desk
where a Windows logo was twinkling off
to untype everything, even this poem.
Faster, faster my already played
days, months, years raced gibbering past.

Glimpsed at Retirement,
a flock of hands in empty gestures
flying apart... Like that stop-gap film
'London to Brighton in five minutes'
I saw the track of my career (friends, enemies
flashing over at points) flickerbook past;
back to a first interview
swallowing like ectoplasm all those busy lies.

Jan Eyck's *'Couple in a Convex Mirror'*
tweaked by Magritte, the wife and I posed
in purple parodies of the Sixties,
bald spot recovering itself
with a Beatles mop, back to our first date.
Meanwhile the children disappeared
like Russian dolls then aniseed balls
into tiny seed-like versions of themselves.

Blurring over the embarrassment
of adolescence, I find myself
kneeling in favourite pearl grey shorts
beside Nannah's wind up gramophone
cranking up Handel to a chipmunk shriek.
Finally, like something on a microwave plate,
myself as foetus waiting to be born...
Then *beep beep beep*. But no one to take it out.

Ultrasound (20 weeks)

Look at you - under a wedge
of grey streaked light
lying on your back
heart darkly pumping,
Mekon skull its jawline showing
seedcorn teeth ready to bud,
spine a flung lariat of pearls,
tossed hoops of your ribs
shining as if radioactive.

What do you gather from outside
this cone of darkness?
Thwumping of heartbeats systolic diastolic?
Each intake of breath an earthquake
whooshing along the bloodstream?
Can you hear giants -
your mother laughing, singing perhaps?
Do you discern shades of darkness
like a Rothko painting, crimson on black?

Outside this half drawn
curtain what kind of universe
awaits? What comedy? What hurts?
Lying there thumb in mouth
on your cushion of amniotic
you remind me of bones I saw once
at the bottom of a pit
in Orkney, under a stone cist.

Newborn

You will remember none of this –
how we loved to pass you around
like a parcel. To wrap, unwrap.
How we marvelled at the newness of your skin,
the softness of a foot that has walked on water,
tiny pearl fingernails.
How we laughed to see you on your back
kicking out like a toy on a stick,
a tipped up beetle, a disco show-off.
How you wore that look of soft amazement
in dawn-blue eyes of not yet colour
wondering at shapes on the window
or the arrangement of ceiling lights.
How we fought for a piece of you -
my earlobe, so-and-so's nose.
How we manoeuvred to pick you up
about the size and weight
of a hot water bottle -
a comfort not for you but for us.
How you heightened our senses
to catch your still breathing,
to nuzzle the fragrance of your scalp
or nose a bouquet of nappy noises
down to the green fingerpaint of your poo.
How loudness could make you flinch,
trapped wind appear to make you smile.
How hiccups were the No. 1 enemy
to be fought, grunting squirmily, against.
None of this will you remember.

Hello Goodbyes

Why do we take such delight
in you, legs bowed like a cowboy
toddling towards us arms out
across a floor tipsy with toys?
So many Firsts: first steps, first 'words',
first efforts with a building block
or with a spoon, splodge-mouthed, to feed yourself.
The wonders of an expanding universe -
ladybird, leaf, moon -
to be named, all magical first times.
Even your wilfulness, furiously shaking your head,
looked on with fondness, pride?

Is it because we feel ourselves tumbling
down the far side of that learning curve?
Beginning to contemplate Last Things...
Last time, knees beginning to twinge,
we tackle a mountain walk?
Last time, lenses fading,
we catch that blue on apricot flash
of a jay as it blurs into the wood?
Beginning to learn (or unlearn?)
that life does not stack up like Lego blocks.
The universe decays. Words fail.
Popsicles kersplat.

So briefly to meet -
you wobbling toward me
to be scooped up, kissed,
me sighing back over your shoulder
through the tickly wisps of your innocence.

Ouch!

says Kitty guiding my hand
to a spot on her knee like a red biro mark.
Ouch she says patting the top of my head
with its scab of baldness
as I kneel to kiss it better, her wounded place.
Yes Big Ouch I say *to my vanity.*
Big Ouch she says pointing for the first time
to the hole in my head where an eye once was.
Big Big Ouch I say *Lucky to get away with that one.*
Big Big Ouch she says showing where a ladybird
wing case splayed like a clockwork toy
lies broken on the sunny morning path.
Yes, that's the biggest ouch of all I think,
postponing the moment when language expands
to explain the kinds and degrees of ouch -
the ouches we suffer but don't let show
on the outside, the ouch of rejection
like a comfort toy we can never re-find,
the ouch of bumps, bangs, bombs and earthquakes
heard on the news we can do nothing about...
O Kitty, so hard to explain
all that threatens to overwhelm
our ouch-time discussion in this sunny garden
with its clematis tendrils, its black and deco bees
fumbling at the upward freckled foxgloves
and you climbing back
on pink push-along Pig
to have another go -
like our planet careering blindly
round its orbit *ouch ouch ouch ouch ouch ouch* –
at the pursuit of butterflies and happiness.

Ultrasound (70 years)

Could be a masseuse
the nurse – strictly pretty...
instructs me to take off my shirt, relax
on a prepared bed of kitchen tissue.
Smearing my lower belly
with cold no nonsense fingers
she takes something like a torch
or karaoke mike,
asks would I care to see the picture?

On a radar screen by my head
hanging from the grey roof of a cave
the thick black rope of my aorta.
Sliding lower she demonstrates
how it divides, one braid to each leg.
Three polyps (luckily benign)
cluster like molluscs on the rock of a kidney
while heaped in the distance
the mud banks of my upper intestine.

All day, guts on display,
I walk through the skin deep world
thinking how frail we are, how frail.
Rubbing against my fellow men
I am careful not to prick their bubbles.
Sensitised to inside out
I hear with new ears
through deep tissues of the world
the call of whales mewling as if in pain.

Next week to school

With peacefulness this afternoon
of warm September seems replete.
Under a sky of cooling blue
a final cube of standing wheat
by chattering combine smoothed away,
each roller bale a harvest moon.
Late swallows fidget on the line
excited to be leaving us behind.

We take our usual Sunday walk
to nowhere much, fingers in mine
hotly insistent, dragging back
to some ditch-side discovery –
wild arum, lights-at-danger sign.
You listen solemnly to what I say
nodding your head, then won't stop
to let me tie your shoe-lace up.

To reach the plumpest blackberry
for you; to kick a skittish stone;
to start on some improbable *'because'*
then catch my shadow on the grass,
a ponderous ape; to be alone
together, trooping quietly;
to carry you when you are tired,
eyelash tickling my beard –

when will such sweetness come again?
They're going to burn the stubble. Look!
Edges of the field turned back.
A bat shape frantics down the lane
as if to pick up something lost.
In my bones a sense of frost
and to the west pink in the air
as if tomorrow were on fire.

9 781911 048282